PSYCHO TAXI BOY

— ON A —

TERRIBLY HOT SUNDAY NIGHT WITH THE SOUTHERN BAPTIST CONVENTION

A COLLECTION OF CHURCH STORIES

DEBRA ROBINSON

DEDICATION

Dedicated to my ragtag collection of way-showers and sacred teachers with special affection for Tom Robbins, wordsmith extraordinaire, and Ipsita Roy Chakraverti who gave me the courage to write my stories.

BIO

Debra Robinson (1951-) has forged an unconventional path through life following the pathless path. From running a hostel on Cape Breton Island, founding Parables bookstore in the wilds of NYC, going on to manufacturing with a human face, going round the world solo at 50 gathering wisdom from many cultures, becoming a Thai Masseuse, healer and spiritual counselor and now, writer.

Contents

What Church do You Attend, Dear?

Often times I am asked by well-meaning Christians and some nosy ones, as well, about my church affiliation.

Sometimes I feel as though I must pass their 'Test' before any further conversation can follow.

I must be pigeon-holed and categorized to be understood. They must know to whom I belong. I can sometimes feel a little judgment coming on…

I am pretty squirmy on this topic. As you get to know me, you will understand why.

"Church" has been a pretty squirmy experience from the start…and I don't just mean the kind of squirming in the pews that we generally do as little children, though that should have been a tip-off.

But I honestly don't have the kind of answer that anyone is particularly pleased with…and I've been working on this for a long time now.

It was never my intention to become the kind of believer that I wound up becoming, but after a while, you know 'the Voice'. And you follow…

Don't worry, I'm not hearing voices…I'm talking about the 'still, small Voice'.

It has been an offbeat journey, to say the least, but it has also been potent and authentic.

That works for me…

But back to the question…

In the kindest, softest way that I can, I tell them that I have come to understand that it's ALL church.

I count myself lucky if they don't quite hear me and move on. But that almost never happens.

"Why, what do you mean?!" they ask with a puzzled expression.

Or… "Oh yes, I believe that, too." (not knowing a thing about what they just said)

"But, WHERE do you GO to church?" they persist. "You HAVE to go somewhere!"

"Well dear heart," I say, "Right here and now, where we stand, is 'Church' even though it's Tuesday at 2:15 pm."

I am already categorized as some sort of heretic or new-ager.

Not good enough, I realize. It's going to be another tricky encounter.

"Well, where do you go on Sunday MORNING?" (as if I'm some idiot child)

By now they have had just about as much nonsense from me as they are willing to take.

Taking my life and what's left of my reputation in my hands, I reply along these lines, "Well... these days I can usually be found at Prairie Creek Reservoir on my pontoon boat."

They are immediately offended, but I also know that deep down they are envious, as well.

Now...if this person attends the so-called megachurch in town, I might follow up with the declaration that I have been hanging out at **God's** megachurch.

And then, depending on how feisty I'm feeling in that moment, I'll continue with "It's just me and the ducks, the herons and fish, just breathing in the fresh

air and watching the water sparkle with sunshine."
"You know…you can really hear God out there…all day long, if you like. How's THAT for a sermon?!" I smile.

They are usually a little flustered by now and will shift to another line of questioning. "Now you know scripture requires you to be in submission to a pastor" to which I reply, "I am under Jesus' authority…is that not sufficient?" (apparently, it's not)

"But you MUST be in submission to a pastor and not forsake the assembling of yourselves together."

"Well now, you may have a point there. I have been searching for a long time for a pastor who knows more than I have come to know in my simple way… one that can bring me closer to God. So far, I haven't found one. Most of the ones I have encountered are more concerned with their programs and budgets and membership drives."

"Oh…and then there is the other matter of finding one who's life is a worthy example. Your new pastor is what now…33 years old? Now why would I go sit under a child? From what I understand of his family life, his life isn't working out so well. If the pastor isn't making his own life work, then why would I sit under him and let him tell me how to make my life work?"

"But you must go somewhere to be fed!" they cry, intent on winning the argument or my soul...I'm not sure which.

"My dear," I reply, "I have been walking with God since I was 22. I am now 60 years old. If I don't know how to feed myself by now, I should be ashamed of myself, don't you think?"

THE 1ST CHURCH OF BOB

After yet another long and arduous search for a place of worship and higher learning, I finally settled on the First Church of Bob.

How one finds a church like this must remain undisclosed, you understand.

Perhaps 'It' finds 'You'. But what works for me would probably never work for you…

Bob is a kind and enquiring soul who has provided a certain sort of education to me. I met him early on in what I call 'The Inner World Tour'.

Backing up a bit, in my fiftieth year, I traveled around the world solo. There is something that comes with being fifty and above…that is, if you are still growing. Life takes on more depth, surprising new vistas, richer magic, more hilarity. That journey stirred up far more questions than it answered…

On my return, I shipped myself off to a spiritualist camp for a different kind of sojourn. I went there to mull things over, do a bit of writing and see if I could get a few answers to my questions.

My plans for a 3 month stay unraveled almost immediately and I found myself in the somewhat embarrassing position of explaining to friends and family just what I was doing years later in this quirky out-of-the-way spot in America's Heartland.

I have sometimes wondered myself...

I told them the most honest thing...that I was now on 'The Inner World Tour'.

The Inner World Tour can be trying at times for there are few reliable roadmaps...and that is where a word of tribute must be given to my mapmakers. They are few.

I have had a ragtag assortment of zany spiritual teachers along the way...

Among them...Psycho Taxi Boy, Deaf Steve who taught me telepathically, Roland "the Kid Next Door," Shirley the reluctant psychic, Patrick (of "Hello My Heart") and 2 Joes (one of whom is described in "Tokyo Joe". Those stories will be found in upcoming collections.)

But when things get really out of hand and I find myself on the most precarious precipice where only Pan and naïve goats would plant a hoof, it is the veritable Tom Robbins who shows me that I am

Still on the Path. I credit much of my sanity to his unorthodox guidance.

"I know my sheep and my sheep mostly know me."

So back to Bob…

Bob was my neighbor at the spiritualist camp. Old Bob had overseen decades of seekers and séances, frauds, fakirs, trance mediums, trumpets floating in air, table- tipping, transfigurations and spirit manifestations of every kind imaginable. Bob had investigated most all of what can be seen in that arena.

He somehow manages to retain a certain compassion for all the foibles carried out in a place like that. He keeps one of the best libraries there, to boot. He became my trustworthy guide to the mysteries along that path…a kind of teacher-in-residence.

And that is how I came to 'The First Church of Bob'.

The FCOB boasts no regular hours of service and is open to all inquirers. Weekdays it is held in the back office of Bob's appliance parts shop. Just walk in the door, pour yourself a cup of coffee and take a well-worn seat.

Above the old coffeemaker is a sign that reads 'Hebrewing all day' which is about the only concession old Bob makes for the Bible. I asked him again recently, "How old were you when you kicked yourself out of the Catholic church?' He repeated the story to me with the same dark relish as before.

You'll have to fish the details from him yourself, but he was about 10 when he had the run-in with the bishop in which some tart words were exchanged.

No collection plate is ever passed around the circle of congregants. Offerings of a can of coffee or a package of Styrofoam cups are accepted if you're a regular. It's ok to bring lunch. It's ok to spend the entire day if you want. Most people come and go according to who they like or dislike in the congregation. Bob is curiously welcoming of all comers...

While you're there, pick up a book, try out the ozone, put questions to Bob about the bicameral mind and the origins of civilization or the search for Omm Seti and off you go for a day of unscripted spiritual finding. Old Bob has been on the path for a fairly long time, even for this life.

As he tells it, things started heating up for him when he was a lad of three or four.
Most nights he would wake in the wee hours to find a group of rather porous-appearing people crowded around the foot of his bed. They watched him, wordlessly, night after night.
Young Bobbie ducked under the covers in fear but found over time that they meant him no harm.

He eventually got a little used to the spirits. He never got to the bottom of that mystery, but he's tackled a few others along the way…

Now you can't get all your Enlightenment in one place, but many fascinating bits and pieces of enlightenment were gathered at the FCOB.

Bob has a few arcane talents that drew me in his direction… For instance, he has a way of scanning a crowd for the one person in it who doesn't fit in. With a detective's eye, he would spot someone wearing antiquated clothing or a hairstyle from another era. Another time it might be someone looking the other way from the action. These people would appear in one moment and disappear in the next. I've seen him do it…a kind of ghost-spotting.

He also has a talent for analyzing handwriting that he learned from old Esther who learned it back in the day when they called it 'grapho-analysis'. Esther was my sprightly, elderly landlady at the spiritualist camp.

I remember the day of our first meeting…
I handed her a check for the rent. A quick glance at the single scribbled initial at the bottom of the check was all she needed to describe my entire relationship with my mother. She did so with impressive accuracy. Given the complexity of said relationship, she was pretty darn good.
(Esther's story is found in "Girl in a Hurry").

Bob does pretty well with hypnosis, too. He turned out to be a good partner in past-life regression escapades.

Given the sensitive nature of those sessions, the reader will have to wait until the Cosmos deems the material appropriate for sharing.

I'm not sure Bob ever got over his early predilection for using hypnosis to get girls, so there came a time to bring that avenue of research to a conclusion.

Most Friday nights, the 1st Church of Bob convened at The 3 Pigs…a throwback era bar and restaurant, replete with burgundy imitation leather banquettes and antique lighting that had seen better days.

The 3 Pigs still served up a good steak and cheap drinks. When so inclined, many a Saturday and Sunday evening were spent there, as well. "Dammit Janet" was our faithful server as we communed over wine and garlic toast. The 3 Pigs was a veritable portal to another time and place and that made it the perfect spot to venture between the worlds.

What conversations we had…We had some formidable debates, too!

An education from an old master that couldn't be gotten in a better way…

I had a relatively good sojourn at the FCOB, that is, up until the time that Bob informed me that I was to be his reward for following the Path of Enlightenment. The problem was that I had not been similarly informed… I was not up for grabs. A classic pitfall between teacher and student…

In a carefully calculated response, I asked Bob when he had converted to Islam.

I was met with a dark scowl. Bob was notoriously anti-religious.

"Virtue is its own reward, Bob… Don't you agree?"

Nothing like mixed motives to mess up a good thing…

And so, once again, after thinking that I had finally found a true teacher, he turned out to be like the others. Seems they were always after your money or your power or your other attributes…

He remains unconvinced…

UNCLE GEORGE

We were on our way to church one night for yet another predictable and disappointing church service.

We were members of Brooklyn's most popular interdenominational church.

But for us, something was missing…something was just not right.

"What was it?' we wondered yet again…

We had tried so many times to get into the spirit of the place…

We couldn't put our finger on what made us so uncomfortable…

Lord knows, everyone else seemed wildly enthusiastic. What misfits we were….

We couldn't fit ourselves in no matter how hard we tried. People were beginning to notice that we hung back a little.

We had discovered that everyone had to be in lock step at all times…or else. The same smiles, the same 'amens', giving assent to every suggestion from the pastor. Right or wrong. No questions allowed. We were beginning to realize that this was not a group that tolerated dissent.

The dissatisfaction we felt was growing.
Each service felt like a fresh assault on our spirits.
That night, as we drove to church for the Wednesday evening service, we finally voiced our deep discomfort.

The question we finally asked ourselves was "What is church?"
Was this God's idea of how it should be?
If so, we were woefully lacking…
We were at an impasse, and something had to give.
We sat silently and waited… We wanted God's input.
We drove slowly and somewhat aimlessly in the direction of the church as we considered the question.

It was a bitterly cold and rainy evening in February.
As the daylight faded, the rain turned to sleet and ice.
The wind was whipping, people were clutching their coats.
It was not a night to be out if you could avoid it.

We found ourselves in a black neighborhood crowded with people at the end of the workday.
We drove slowly, observing the scene, when we suddenly spotted an old black man weaving his way through the crowd, clad only in pajamas and bedroom slippers.
We watched in shock as people rushed by, pretending not to see him.
He was being jostled and pushed aside by the commuters rushing home for the evening.

We simply couldn't believe that no one would extend a hand to help this elderly man.

Maybe they thought he was drunk.
The cars behind us were honking and pushing us along, so we circled the block hoping that by the time we got back to that corner, he would be gone-hoping that someone would have looked after him.
When we finally got back to the corner we found him again, stumbling badly now and being shoved by the still unseeing crowds.

Where had we seen that behavior before?
We realized with a little catch in our throats… after our church services!
The church we attended was situated in a poor neighborhood.
As we left services each time, there would be a few homeless people standing outside asking for a bit of help.
The church folks would callously push past them, sometimes with a shove or a harsh word.
They were rushing off to their favorite cheesecake restaurant where they would invariably stuff themselves.
The servers hated to see them coming. Their mistreatment of the servers was legendary. They'd run the staff ragged all evening.
It was always the same thing…how much could they get for nothing?
They often complained until they got a free meal.

In the end they might leave a bit of small change for tips.

Their behavior stood in such stark contrast to the message they professed.

We were embarrassed to be seen with them after a few such encounters.

We soon shed those thoughts and focused on the scene in front of us.

Suddenly our man stumbled and fell into a filthy, storm-clogged gutter.

Still, no one seemed to notice!

We maneuvered our little Volkswagen to the curb and jumped out.

We lifted the old man to his feet and half-dragged him to the car.

He was nearly frozen. He was incoherent and shivering intensely.

He was in bad shape from exposure to the cold and sleet.

We tried in vain to find out who he was and where he needed to go.

He carried no ID. He could not speak. His condition was pitiful. So we just concentrated on getting him warmed up.

He was not drunk, but beyond that, we couldn't piece together his situation.

We searched for a policeman but couldn't find one.

We were at a loss in a strange neighborhood with a nameless, homeless man in tow.

We realized that we would have to come up with a solution ourselves.

Once seated in a warm car, our fellow was coming around slowly.
We found a diner and got some hot soup for our guest.
Offering him some hot food stirred him and he showed the first signs of life.
He shivered so much that he couldn't hold the container or feed himself, so we fed him carefully.
After a few spoonfuls of soup, he nodded off and slept a bit. His shivering slowly subsided.
We drove aimlessly for a while just to thaw him out and figure out our next move. He started to come to after about an hour, but we still couldn't get a word from him. No name, no address, no explanation. We drove around and around feeling pretty helpless.

And then our man made a sudden move.
He jerked his head up and clumsily pointed to the right with a grunt. That was all.
So we headed right. Then after awhile, he sat up and motioned to the left. Off we went to the left! Then he nodded off again.
This was repeated a few more times until we finally realized that we were going in hopeless circles.
We were no closer to a destination of any kind and to make matters worse, we were now lost in an unfamiliar part of Brooklyn on a dark and stormy night.

Our passenger obviously didn't know who he was or where he lived.
Now what!?

As we threaded our way through the area, we found a block of brownstone houses.
It was a quiet residential street…a place where we could pause for a few moments out of traffic.
Finally, I said, 'Stop the car'.
I got out and headed for the first house with a porch light.
I knocked on the door and waited, feeling a little fear and a lot of frustration.

A tall stately grey-haired black woman answered the door. She towered over me, obviously wondering what a white girl was doing knocking on her door after nightfall.

I tried to explain to her that I had an old man in pajamas with no known identity in my possession and that I needed to use a phone, PLEASE….

She drew herself up to her full height and questioned me closely.

Where had we found him? What was he doing? What did he look like? What was he wearing?

Suddenly, she gave a shriek and cried "Uncle George!"
I stepped back, startled…

She dashed inside, grabbed a coat and ran past me down the steps into the street to our car.
I followed her, still uncomprehending.

When she reached our passenger, she launched into an emotional tirade.
"Uncle George!!! What got into you that you would leave the hospital!!!??"

This WAS, in fact, HER Uncle George! I shook my head in disbelief!

Meanwhile, poor Uncle George was getting the scolding of a lifetime.

It turned out that Uncle George had been taken to King's County Hospital that morning with a stomach complaint.
As near as anyone could tell, he had waited hour after hour for someone to see him. Toward the end of the day, he simply got hungry and frustrated and just left on his own.
He was going to walk back home. He was a bit senile and confused and lost his way.
He had been missing for hours…and now, in some inexplicable way, he was home.

We were all amazed at what had just taken place!
His grateful niece thanked us and hurried him inside, scolding all the way!

As we headed back toward the church, we checked our watches.

We had been gone for more than 2 hours.

Church would be letting out just about the time we would be arriving.

It was hardly worth the trip now, we realized. We might as well head home.

We were actually kind of relieved to have missed church that night.

We turned the corner and headed toward home when suddenly, the atmosphere in that little car shifted slightly.

There was a Presence…soft, but sure.

And the revelation that came to us held the answer to our all-but-forgotten question…the one we had asked earlier that evening.

"This is Church," the Voice said. "THIS is Church…"

My Police Record

Seems like everyone around me these days has a police record....
What gives, I wondered?
What's up with that?!
My record is basically lily white and at my age and temperament, it is likely to stay that way.
Or so I thought...

As I pondered this oddity, it came to me, a bit belatedly, that I actually had had a couple of early run-ins with the law!
I actually had a police record! I, indeed!
So much for thinking I was above the rest.
Once more, the joke was on me...

Now, this was not a record that a criminal would be proud of...
Oh No...not at all!

And so, donning the lens of judiciary perception,
I began to recall a rather lengthy and disorderly
history of run-ins with the law that I had

conveniently banished to the recesses of my sub-
conscious.

I'm pretty sure, given the time span involved, that I
can no longer be held accountable for these crimes
due to the statute of limitation laws.

So, it is safe to confess my crimes at long last.
The list runs as long as my 8-year-old arm.

I started out breaking out of jail at the earliest
opportunity…jail being my parents' home.
I would sneak back in for meals and sleep, but I
needed to be certain at all times that I could break
free again. I had places to go…things to do!

From time to time, I would get caught.
I gave my folks a terrible fright now and then!
They would put their heads together in an effort to
contain me.
They installed more and better locks, they reinforced
windows, doors-the works!
I made it my business to outwit them at every turn.

I practiced constantly, honing my skills, primarily
those of disguise, such as wearing my mother's
dresses and heels, subterfuge (I could spell it at that
tender age, accepting bribes of candy from the
night shift factory workers with whom I visited

in the pre-dawn hours, duplicity, and breaking and entering upon my return.

My criminal behavior escalated, however, when I followed the milk delivery van by our house very early one morning. Thinking that I might bribe my folks with a gift of milk, if caught, and mimicking my mom's borrowing of a cup of sugar, etc. from the lady next door, it seemed reasonable enough to borrow the neighbor's milk jug.

The theft of that milk bottle landed me in the emergency room with shards of evidence embedded in my arms after I fell forward from the weight of it. The punishment seemed to fit the crime and I was released with a stern warning.

There was a period of peace after that…even reform, once the nuns got hold of me in Catholic school… the Penitentiary of earliest reckoning.

But, as I said, I was reforming myself pretty handily. I had made a bold turnaround and was bent on becoming Saint Debbie before something worse could happen.

But it wasn't long before I found myself in the back of a police cruiser, headed back to jail once again!

"Er…Mr. and Mrs. Rouse? Is this your daughter?"
intoned the burly officer.
Wide-eyed and gape-mouthed, my folks alternately
glared at me and made confused gesticulations
toward the good officer.
They had no idea that I was pounding pavement at
5am on a frosty Green Bay morning.

"I was just on my way to church!" I cried woefully.
"Was that against the law?!"
Apparently, I appeared to be on the slippery edge of
somebody's law!
Discussions regarding jurisdiction ensued!

Whose law prevailed? The city ordinances, my folks
or God's?
They, being unprepared for this level of complexity,
faltered ever so briefly.
There was a moment's pause-a costly mistake,
from which I snatched the victory!
From that time forward, my folks had to let me
attend 5:45 am daily Mass and the police agreed to
keep an eye out for me.

From time to time, my patience and my parents'
exasperation were tested when an officer, new to the
beat, would pick me up for questioning and the
scene would be repeated at my parents' house.

But, each time, the law held firm.

Keeping my record clean these days…

Wednesday Night Seduction... Pimping for the Preacher

This incident caught me unaware, even after all I'd learned from hard experience…

Often when I was travelling, I would visit a church service.
More often than not, I would seek out an Assemblies of God Church.
They felt safe and welcoming. I found them to be more earnest and sincere than many others.

I had found along the way that many non-denominational churches could be creepy. Someone would invariably be drawn to me, hungry for more than fellowship.
I had learned to keep some distance, sad to say…
I seated myself toward the back of the sanctuary and kept to myself, as usual.
I was just passing through. There was no need to get to know these people or be involved. I wouldn't be filling out a visitor's card or answer any personal questions.
I would just slip in and out without anyone noticing me. I was just there to worship. The service was

typical for a Wednesday evening Nothing to get excited about, but sufficient. It was good enough for the occasion.

As I was slipping out of the church as the service concluded, I was surprised to find a woman pursuing me to my car. She rather anxiously introduced herself as the church secretary. She noted that I was a newcomer and wanted to welcome me back.

I thanked her and explained that I was just passing through.

That should have been enough…

She pressed me further, explaining that the pastor had taken special notice of me and had sent her to invite me for tea with the two of them…just a hand of fellowship since I might be feeling alone on the road.

I wasn't especially inclined to do that sort of thing, but you never know…it could be an interesting hour.

She was visibly relieved when I said yes.

She quickly offered to have me ride with them since I was unfamiliar with their town.

I just as quickly replied that I would rather take my own car.

I wondered why I was so quick and emphatic…
I appeared distrustful of them.

She tried again…fairly insisting.

I stuck to my guns on instinct…but questioned
and criticized myself for my independent, resistant
attitude. I told myself I should be more friendly…
more Christian.

I had fallen short again. Too late. I couldn't help myself.

She looked disappointed, but she gave in finally.

I followed them to the restaurant. Introductions were
made, we ordered tea and pie and we chatted lightly
for a few minutes while we waited for our dessert.

Then the secretary excused herself for a moment to
take a phone call.

She hurried back and informed us that she needed to
go home right away to take care of a family emergency.
She would just catch a cab…not to worry, she told
'Pastor John'.

She rushed out the door with apologies.

I felt a moment's discomfort as I sat across from the
minister. This was not the arrangement that I had
anticipated.

I tried to assure myself that everything was alright, but I felt strangely uncomfortable.

I chalked it up to my general shyness and nervousness around men.

I tried to quell my feelings.

After all…it doesn't get much safer than an Assemblies pastor.

I could not have been more wrong! Little did I anticipate the events that followed…

All of a sudden, the pastor reached across the table and took my arm as he started to tell me how lonely he was, how he needed a godly wife, how he had noticed me from the pulpit. His pressure on my arm increased and in moments, I was held in a grip from which I could not escape. Then with his other hand he reached for my leg under the table and I realized in horror that he was groping me under my skirt!

His face remained impassive, friendly…he was practiced at this!

By now he was leaving bruises on my arm, letting me know there would be no escape.

I was paralyzed with shock, unable to speak or move, yet I knew that I had to break away before anything worse happened.

Thank God I had come in my own car! I would have been at his mercy if I hadn't.

When I looked in his eyes I saw a kind of madness and frenzy.

It chilled me to the bone!

He was like a ravening monster…in shepherd's clothing.

That did it! My anger finally broke through my fear! There was no second guessing what was going on now!

This was not a lonely man! This was a predator!

Suddenly my mind started working again. My adrenaline surged, my mind cleared and I knew what to do next.

I forced myself to relax, smiled at him and went limp for a moment…just long enough for him to let his guard down and think I might go along with his plan. In the next moment, I gave a furious wrench of my arm and broke free of his grip.

I ran for the door in such a way that he would not dare follow in sight of all the surprised diners. I ran to my car, locked myself in, started the engine and raced out of sight. Then I parked in a safer place, turned off the headlights and pulled myself together.

Why had this happened to me?

How exactly did I fall prey to this?

I felt so betrayed…so violated.
It was like a snatch and grab or a hit and run accident.
'No!' I realized moments later. Nothing about what had just happened was accidental!
It was every bit intentional!

As the pieces of the puzzle fell into place, I realized that they had set me up.
At the pastor's instigation, his secretary played her part in the scheme.
A trap had been set for me…
He spotted me, alone and a stranger, innocent, possibly vulnerable.
Hard to trace, likely to move on in shocked silence…

And that is what I did unfortunately…

I cannot recall the name of the church or its location. In those early days I was still recovering and too weak to do more than ensure my own self-preservation.

Today I would tell you where it took place. I would name names to help protect other unsuspecting women and parishioners.

It was subtle in the moment…but so obvious later.
As I thought about it, it became clear that they had worked hand in hand like this many times. She played her part flawlessly. A wave of revulsion swept over me.
How could a woman be duped into such a thing?! A church secretary, no less…
What kind of hideous denial was she in? How could a pastor be so depraved?
How does a person live with himself and continued to call himself a man of God?!

I would like to say that this was an isolated instance, but in the years that followed, I have discovered many such unholy alliances.

Foolish women guarding the fort for pedophiles, gay pastors with unsuspecting wives and families, cheating, alcoholic, thieving shepherds of blind sheep

They are charged with threatening off all intruders, aiding and abetting their cover-ups.

One church secretary I know was told in rather stark terms that "Your job is to make me look good!" Her pastor remains one of the worst offenders at large.

Why did she blind herself to all that she had seen over the years?

"Well," she said, "when my husband was sick, he asked the congregation to take up a collection to help with our medical expenses".

"Oh, I see."

For this, she overlooks gay sex, infidelity, coercion, blackmail, pedophilia, drug use and more...much more. She rather proudly, if not foolishly, vaunts herself as the great pastor's personal assistant.

There are none so blind as those who will not see...

Deeetroit Choir

As improbable as it may seem, this is another true story…

One early winter I travelled to visit my new friend in Detroit.

We had met the summer before when he stayed at my hostel on Cape Breton.

This young man had experienced a very beautiful… and unexpected…spiritual awakening there.

It was deep and transformative, revealing a very wise and tender-hearted soul.

He had recently become a Christian. I knew he had a tough road ahead of him.

I wanted to see how he was getting along and, in turn, he had asked me to help him find a church to attend.

I was always ambivalent about that sort of thing.

I hated to see someone like this young man make a good start in his spiritual life and then get caught up in a dead church.

Time and time again, once a church got a hold of a new convert, they would misappropriate and 'educate' the Life right out of them.

Still, most people would feel the need of the support of a body of believers.

It just helped to show them how to navigate the scene…

My young friend and I would look for a church on Sunday morning.
But this was Saturday night and we opted for a long walk to talk and get caught up on everything. We walked for miles, lost in conversation, until we found ourselves on the mean streets of downtown Detroit. The city was in serious decline by then with boarded-up storefronts covered in menacing graffiti. By the time we reached downtown the sun was going down, the temperature was dropping fast and the atmosphere was anything but welcoming.

It was a long walk back and we needed to get warmed up before we made the return trip. We looked for a diner or coffee shop, but every place was closing and the downtown was rapidly emptying of people. It was too late to turn back and unwise to go forward. But, as luck would have it, we eventually chanced upon a building with an open door and a brightly-lit interior.
We ducked inside, hoping to warm up a bit and rest before the long trek home.
We found ourselves in a stately old building, quite at odds with its surroundings in the deteriorating downtown area.
Once inside, we were fascinated by the rich architectural details. We wandered through halls leading to grand rooms, admiring the old carved staircase, the ornate tiles, intricate designs and marble wall panels.

The place reminded me of a turn-of-the-century Masonic temple.

We headed up the staircase to see what the mezzanine and the balcony held.

We had been chattering away excitedly up to that point, but when we reached the balcony and surveyed the auditorium below, we quickly lowered our voices. Down below us, we saw a few elderly black folks entering the building.

They were carrying Bibles under their arms. Apparently, the lodge had been turned into a church and we had intruded on their service.

We sat down straightaway and tried to be as inconspicuous as possible.

The handful of people gathering were thinly dispersed around the huge room.

A few more arrived. There were perhaps a dozen or so worshippers scattered throughout that grand auditorium. They were mostly older, mostly women. They bowed their heads and prayed quietly or spoke in low tones while they waited for the service to start. Two or three more people joined them and then their prayer service began.

Not a very impressive gathering. No pastor or leader among them. Just a simple gathering of humble black folks, heads bowed as they prayed quietly. We sat as still we could, hoping no one would notice our presence.

After a time, a voice was raised…and then another.

The people began to pray out loud.
They prayed informally, each tending to their own concerns.
Before long, everyone had risen to their feet…all of them praying out loud.
It was a bit strange…all these discordant voices.

As they prayed, their prayers grew more fervent, more animated.
Then I heard a woman begin to pray in tongues… glossolalia…other languages. I'd had some experience of that myself, but I wondered what my young friend would think of it. We had never talked about anything like that. Soon another worshipper lifted her voice and prayed in tongues.
And another…and another. Soon all joined in.
Before long, there was an embarrassing cacophony of sound.

Then one of the women lifted her voice above the others and began to sing in tongues.
I had never heard anything like it!
It was an eerie tongue and melody.
Her voice was strong and beautiful…confident and full-throated.

Then the others began to sing in tongues, as well.
The sound was utterly confusing as they each sang different songs in different languages.

Their voices became louder now and more emphatic.

I was embarrassed, not knowing what to say to my
friend.
But then suddenly, in the proverbial 'twinkling of an
eye,' the most astonishing thing happened!

Their voices suddenly became ONE
The most glorious song was heard…
It was beautiful beyond what words
can express.!
And again suddenly, the entire dome reverberated
with many hundreds, perhaps thousands, of voices
…an invisible angelic choir.

The music we heard was incomparably beautiful.
It is so far beyond what can even be imagined here.
There is nothing on earth that it can be compared to.
It lifted us to our feet.
We stood frozen with our hair standing on end,
transported into what can only be described as a
heavenly realm.

Tears streamed down our faces. We were unable to
speak.

Our eyes alone confirmed to each other that we
were hearing the same other-worldly performance.
The hall was filled-to- overflowing with voices
singing in majestic tones.
The sound of their voices rose and fell and rose

and fell together for some time.
We stood transfixed in ecstasy...no other world existed.

And then...

Just as suddenly as they had begun, their voices rose and fell one last time and they came to rest as one.

The Silence left us breathless...

Holiness had intermingled with this humble congregation.

A few moments of silence followed. Then without fanfare or remark, the people quietly gathered their things, put on their coats and left for home.

Ladies Lingerie

*A*nderson, Indiana.

The old Walmart was the scene of strange activity....

submitted by eyewitness 'Wild at Heart'.

3:33 am Sunday morning…

I suddenly sat up straight in bed, startled out of a deep sleep for no apparent reason.

It was strange how vividly awake and aware I felt.

I knew that there would be no more sleep.

I wondered what was going on. I felt a visceral sense of urgency.

I dressed quickly and headed downstairs, wondering what I would do with all that time.

Once downstairs, I felt an urge to get into my car and drive to town, an unlikely thing to do on a chill winter morning.

I felt rushed along- hurried out of my own house.

I was a bit disgruntled getting ejected from my warm bed and cozy home at such an early hour.

Once I was driving, I tried to figure out where I would go.

Let's see…what was open? A couple of 24 hr. restaurants, a few gas stations and Walmart.

I had no desire to eat, no desire to shop, but I felt a slight leaning toward Walmart.
What would I do there? There was nothing that I needed…
Then it kind of hit me. 'Well…one always needs new underwear…'
When I got to the store, I parked amid a scant handful of cars and headed inside.
It was predictably deserted at that hour.
I made my way across the store to ladies' lingerie.

What I found there proved to be anything but predictable…
There was a veritable swarm of men!
They had commandeered the whole department!
I slowed way down trying to take in the scene.
There were 10 or 12 men, ranging from about 16 years old to 80.
They were fanned out among the racks of bras and panties…
They circled slowly, lingering in a curious way…not speaking to one another.

However, I soon realized that there was plenty of communication of another kind…
I spied one young man running his fingers slowly along the lines of a lacy black bra while gazing seductively over his shoulder at a middle-aged man.

Another man was twerking panties over his backside while trying to capture the attention of another man who was vying for yet another man's attention.

They were all preening and prancing around in an awkward little dance of male seduction. Ugh!
What was more concerning were the wedding bands that most of them wore.
I wondered about the wives and children who slept innocently in their beds while their husbands and fathers were trolling the lingerie aisles at Walmart at this ungodly hour.
Ungodly, indeed…

I decided to approach the area anyway, not willing to be intimidated by them.
It WAS the women's section, after all.
But when I was discovered, I felt what can only be described as a force field surrounding them. It almost knocked me backwards.
I was NOT wanted there.
And they were NOT about to give up their space or their game.
They were defiant and highly annoyed that a woman would step into what was now their domain. I endured several very hateful, angry glares.
They were furious at having their game intruded upon.
I walked away, but soon decided to double back in an inconspicuous way.

It was all clear to me now...Why I had been woken from sleep, urged to dress and drive to Walmart to get undies, of all things...
What was I to make of what I encountered?

I continued to watch them from behind a pillar.
This was definitely gay behavior, but there was something about them that didn't fit the scene.
I have lived in NYC and Atlanta and had seen plenty of the lifestyle and the players.
They didn't have the look, somehow...
On the other hand, they were all curiously uniform in their appearance.
There was something about their stilted manner...
They HAD a 'look'.
Short flattop haircuts, Sunday morning suits, polished shoes, faintly effeminate personas-the emasculated pseudo-Christian.
It hit me. They had an unmistakable look, alright!
They had the conservative evangelical Christian look.
My stomach twisted...

Leading double lives...in this tawdry display at Walmart.
I could hear them as they left their beds that morning... 'Sleep in, dear. I'll go get the Sunday paper, orange juice and doughnuts. Home soon!'

I waited, I watched and then I'd had enough.
I marched into the department, uttered a few choice words and chased them out. I broke up their party,

blasted them out of their trances and scattered them in all directions, shaming them all the way.
They were incensed, irate!
I didn't care.
I wasn't done with them.

I gave them no opportunity to regroup…this show was over!
Then they acted indignant-suddenly innocent and above reproach!

They finally started leaving the store, heads hung glumly.
I monitored the escape route, heading to the aisles that held orange juice, milk and doughnuts.
There I found the last little huddle of 2 elderly males toying with a teenage boy.

When I stepped between them and asked them which church they attended, they dropped their things and bolted.

Psycho Taxi Boy on a Terribly Hot Sunday Night with the Southern Baptist Convention

"**W**ant to go for a ride? We haven't talked in awhile…"
I recognized that drawl…

Mike Bacon…miscreant, Atlanta Chess Champion cum gypsy cab driver…
Against my better judgment, I said ok.
"Meet me out front in half an hour."
The uniquely infuriating Mike Bacon aka Psycho Taxi Boy…
Our last big blowup was 5 or 6 months before.
He had insulted me to the limits of my patience… over some alleged scandalous behavior of church leaders.

Now Michael had no patience for religious types.
I had little myself, but he had brought his point home in a stunningly dreadful way.
Now, word for word, no one on the planet has a better command of the English language than a denizen of the American South.

They are easily the most colorful, artful and entertaining of the speakers.
They certainly do the most with the least.
Homespun wit and native intellect merge in a wickedly punchy brew.
Consider the likes of Tom Robbins if you don't believe me...

Having ferried all manner of people from around the world in his cab all those years, Michael had an endless supply of quirky stories.
Ever the acute observer of the human condition, driving cab allowed him to travel the world from the comfort of his front seat...affording him not only a unique education, but the freedom to compete in chess tournaments around the country and still keep a roof over his head. We had met in his cab, in fact.
It was Halloween night, but that is another story...

Michael had surmised that I was still somewhat in the chokehold of old time religion and needed some wising up.
There was nothing defensible in religion, according to Michael.
We debated the topic hotly one more time.
He told me exactly why he had no faith in those hypocrites.
Michael waxed virulent that day and we blasted apart.
I was still stinging from his attack months later...

Mike claimed that the most lucrative night of the year for Atlanta's cabbies was the last night of the Southern Baptist convention.

After sending their families and attendees away in time for Sunday services back home, a select group of pastors, choir directors, youth leaders and the like stayed on for a little private convening of their own... at the infamous Cheetah strip club.
Now the only strip club that was open on a Sunday night was the Cheetah.
Cab load after cab load of these church guys were ferried from their fancy midtown hotels to the club all night long.
Mike went into shocking and sordid detail, much to my horror and dismay.
He just wouldn't let up!
Tempers flared!
I didn't care if I ever saw Michael again!

Then the soft drawl of his voice that late afternoon... Much as I hated to admit it, I missed him...his surly, recalcitrant humor, his edgy droll outlook, not to mention the peculiar metaphysical experiences that spontaneously erupted whenever we got together...

I got in the passenger seat alongside Mike, unsure of how to reconnect. He was a little tucked inside, as well. He drove toward downtown Atlanta in silence. Then a little cautious chit chat. Things eased up. It was good spending time with him again.

First stop…one of the most expensive hotels in the heart of midtown.

Three well-dressed gentlemen got into the back seat.
Destination: the Cheetah club.
Mike dutifully dropped them off, wishing them a good night.
Moments later, 2 men emerged from the club with hookers on their arms.
They drunkenly waved Michael down and squeezed in.
The cab suddenly reeked of alcohol, cigar smoke and cheap perfume.
Repugnant! I rolled my window down.
Destination: the hotel we had just come from.
I squirmed uncomfortably.
There was too much activity in the back seat for me, but Michael was unfazed.
Finally, they exited the cab, only to be replaced by another clump of men filling the back seat once more, nervously requesting the Cheetah. They didn't seem the type, but looks could be deceiving, I reasoned. None of them seemed the type, but perhaps I was naïve.

Upon their exit, three pale, overweight drunk guys clambered into the back seat…all sporting wedding bands.
Back to the nice hotel.
The men were foul-mouthed…pretty vile, actually.
I glanced at Mike a few times, wincing at their remarks.

He remained impassive.
'It is what it is,' I could almost hear him say.

As the night wore on, the fares were rowdier, more crude.
The same sickening circuit.
Too many scantily-clad women draped over their fat arms.
Then some lines of cocaine were snorted in the back seat.
I was churning inside, wondering how I could escape the cab.
I'd had enough!
The men were nothing short of bestial, despite their fine suits, expensive watches and other ostentatious trappings of wealth.
I overheard their conversations. There was no escaping it.
I was already mortified, but things were about to get worse...
A snatch of conversation held me riveted.

The men were bragging about their conquests, each one trying to best the others. That's when I heard them mocking their wives...their mistresses...and their congregations!

My blood boiled, my stomach turned...I realized what night it was...Sunday night- the infamous last night of the Southern Baptist Convention.

The fine suits, conservative haircuts, wedding bands, their coarse mockery, the long line of cabs making the non-stop circuit between the Cheetah and the fine hotels.

"Michael! Please get me out of here!!!"
Michael finished one more run…for emphasis.
Then he pulled to the side of the road so I could retch.
I shook with revulsion…and understanding.
He had exposed the rabble of southern Baptist preachers.

checkmate…

CLOSING PRAYER...
POINT CROSS

This is an early story…
Not long after I arrived on Cape Breton, a kindly old man offered me the use of his old summer house. The family used it as their fish camp. Rent-free, he offered as he handed me the key.
I think he sensed that I needed a place to rest for awhile.
He was right.
And so began a sojourn of nearly 10 years.

The old house, though plain and rustic, was charmingly situated between the ocean and the mountains.
I spent a few days tidying it up and making it my own.
I was struck by the peacefulness and beauty of the place.
I needed some time away from people and this seemed the perfect place to be.
The nearest village was 4 miles away, the nearest neighbor ¼ mile away.
I couldn't believe my good fortune.

But of course, nothing is ever as it seems….

Just as I was settling down with a cup of hot tea and my travel diary, there was a sharp knock at the door. Well, not exactly a knock …it was more of a crashing in of the door.

I sat up with a jerk, frightened as the door flew open and a wild-looking young man with a bushy head of black curls strode into my living room.

He forthrightly introduced himself as Roland… Roland Aucoin.

My neighbor from down the hill.

"And who might you be?" he asked.

He then proceeded to pepper me with questions for the next hour as my tea grew cold. I was both fascinated and exasperated by my friendly intruder.

There was a brief pause in our conversation where I actually thought he might leave. But no…

He then cajoled me into taking a hike into the nearby woods.

He promptly enlisted himself as my personal guide to all things Cheticamp.

He told stories by the hour of the old folks and the old ways of this fascinating community. Slowly I was being drawn into their world, so unlike my own.

It was, in many ways, a welcome distraction from the world that I had left.

There was, however, a subtle sense that I was being primed for something with all these stories…a slight sense of urgency and need.

Many hours later, my new friend Roland left for home.

My head was fairly spinning from the barrage of information.

There would be no writing today.

I boiled some fresh water for tea and finally sat down to reflect on my curious visitor and the unexpected turn my day had taken.

Though the stories were charming, I felt somewhat disturbed for reasons I could not define.

I felt like Roland had somehow become a fixture in my life.

That was soon to be confirmed.

Early the next morning my door came crashing open again without warning.

Young Roland had planned a whole day of activities for us.

I tried to protest, but he looked so stricken at the idea that I had planned to spend a quiet day by myself, that I caved in and went along with his plans.

It would be awhile before I realized how isolated these people were and how much they craved contact with the outside world.

But it was more than contact that they craved…

To my unpracticed eye, all was well.

These people lived a life that many would envy.

Beautiful countryside, simple lifestyles, and tranquil circumstances…

Idyllic by most standards.

But my indoctrination had just begun…

As the first weeks passed, I was having a hard
time carving out any quiet time for myself.

It seemed that Roland was at my door every time the
lights were turned on. It didn't matter the hour. Five
or even six times a day he could be counted on to
come crashing in.

I tried living in the dark for awhile…
I thought I might turn the lock on the door as a
means of training him to knock first, but I found
to my consternation that there was no lock on the
door. There was only a small rectangle of old wood
on the outside of the door held in place with a single
nail in the center that served as a lock when one left
the house.
When I tried to tell Roland that I craved a little
privacy and would he please knock first, he was
completely uncomprehending

That's not how things were done here.
Frayed nerves and all, I would have to try to adapt to
their strange society.

As Roland burrowed his way into my life, he started
to share some of the darker aspects of his life with
me. I sensed that he had a lot to unload.

I listened patiently. Before long he brought a young
friend and then a few others, each in turn sharing
their lives and problems with me.

My short-lived dream of the perfect setting was coming undone.

This was a troubled community, and the causes were myriad.

Apparently, I was the safe stranger.
In a village where everyone knew everyone's business, the keeping of secrets was essential.

The young people could come to my house and share the unspeakable.
As in many isolated communities, there was long-standing abuse of many kinds. Alcoholism, domestic abuse, incest, and perhaps, worst of all, clergy abuse. There were frightening layers of darkness and stories that decried belief.

What had I gotten myself into?

Over the next several months, hardly a day went by without the shy intrusions of several young people. Then a few of the older ones came calling as well.

So many stories, so much pain of longstanding.
I was hardly able to do more than listen, but that seemed sufficient for the moment somehow.
I had my own problems to attend to... my own very recent wounds.

I was finding comfort in scripture and in long walks along the ocean shore and the quiet hills.

Many things had conspired to bring me to this place.

For all the interruptions and distractions, it was a place of healing for me.

The wind, the salt air and the simple demands of daily living enacted their healing, each in turn. Carrying water from the well, chopping wood to cook and to keep warm. Unfamiliar tasks for a small-town American girl.

It was Roland who taught me how to build a fire and keep it going through the night. People coming to visit brought small gifts from the garden, some fresh fish, an armload of wood, a loaf of still-warm bread. I needed them as much as they needed me.

It was an unlikely scheme for healing, but it was the perfect one.
In a few short months I had gone from my sad and broken condition to feeling alive and hopeful again. I reveled in my newfound freedom and in this complete change of lifestyle.
I had escaped (literally) from an abusive marriage to a dangerous preacher's kid. I had experienced firsthand the dangers that came of submission to a twisted and heavy-handed gospel.

After my escape, I wanted nothing to do with God, much less his self-appointed representatives.

I had turned my back on all of it.

Much to my surprise, however, I began to feel and experience a gentle presence in my life. I knew that I had been guided to this place.

Moreover, in my first three days here, I had been given a roof over my head, a job and all the makings of a new life.

Things were unfolding for me and the others in fascinating ways.

We were helping and being helped to heal each other.

Before long I had a houseful of young people every night, sometimes long into the night.

Their problems were beyond my help. So I began to share bits of scripture, mostly proverbs, with them.

We tried to decipher what we could.

It seemed to help.

Every week a few more kids would join the group.

Soon we went from having casual discussions to embarking on an actual class.

The first evening there were 14 or 15 young people crowded into my small living room.

One young girl stood out from the others. She was very somber and obviously religious. It was rumored that she planned to join the convent one day.

The 'regular' kids looked up to her in awe.

No problems-this one. Miss Perfect. One less sad story for me to hear.

During the class she was unusually attentive.

It was a good evening's discussion, just like all the others.
At the end we all knelt in a circle holding hands as we said a closing prayer. While we were praying I glanced around the room and noticed that the young girl was swaying back and forth strangely.
Moments later her head fell backward and she began to moan.
At first I thought she was ill.

Suddenly there was a chill in the air, a slight but palpable shift.
In the next moment, a feeling of menace and fear was felt in the room.
Her moans became louder and more guttural.
Soon we heard a man's voice coming from her mouth, cursing and ugly.
The two young people that were holding hands with her withdrew in fear.
Things quickly escalated. Then she began to foam at the mouth.
We were frozen in shock.

Who was this child? What was happening to her?
At first, I thought it was a seizure, but that idea was quickly dispelled.
The voice that emanated from her carried unusual power.
Its terrible presence soon filled the room.
Some of the young people were crying.

I stood up and told them to gather on the opposite side of the room. I gave them instructions to stay together and keep praying.
Once they were gathered together, I turned and walked toward the girl, unsure of what I would do or say.
As I approached I felt something incredible rise up in me.
It was as if Jesus himself rose up inside me and took over.
A bright shining strength… A fierce clarity and intelligence…
I stood before her and a few terse words came out of my mouth…a command.
I cannot recall what words were spoken. It was not me speaking.
In the next moment the young girl's body stiffened and rose to full height.
She then gave a sharp cry and collapsed on the floor with a terrible thud.
She moved slightly on the ground and then fell into a dead sleep.
The awful presence left the room.
We waited quietly. About half an hour passed.

She finally stirred and woke up as if from a bad dream.
You could immediately see the difference in her.
Gone was the strained appearance and religious intensity.
In its place was the soft face of the 12 year old girl that she was.

I had just witnessed the casting out of a demonic spirit.

In this day and age?!

I couldn't believe it but I also couldn't deny it.

But how could this sweet young girl be possessed by something so ugly?

And how could someone so religious be hiding something so terrifying?

I pored over the gospel accounts and read everything I could find regarding casting out spirits.

I was learning in retrospect.

A systematic study showed that Jesus often cast out spirits in the synagogue. Those were the most confusing examples.

Jesus would enter a synagogue and someone would greet him with praise.

He turned to the person praising him and cast a demon out.

I couldn't understand those stories and so I skipped over them.

But I was drawn back to the paradox again and again. Gradually I began to see that demons took many forms, not all of them outwardly evil. Many of them were found in churches and synagogues.

They were outwardly pious, but they were, in fact, impostors.

Religious demons. Hiding in the cleverest of disguises.

This was to be the first of several such encounters.

How did Jesus know when he was dealing with a demon?

How was I to know? It had to do with his discernment.

Discernment is probably the most important as well as the most lacking spiritual gift. I cannot tell you how many times and in how many pulpits I have seen these devils at work. We sense/ recognize one another immediately.

They do not easily give up their power over their congregations.

They are often the most sanctimonious and charming of all.

But they are evil workers nonetheless, bent on manipulation and control of the hearts, bodies, minds and pocketbooks of their naïve victims.

There is a peculiar evil delight taken by those demons who rule over churches. Selah…

It wasn't long before word spread about what was going on in our evening meetings. Hearts were being opened and lives were being changed.

I knew what the word of God had done for me. Now I was seeing its effect on these young people. Our group was growing steadily.

I hitchhiked to Halifax and obtained some Catholic New Testaments from the Bible Society for them. They were eagerly snapped up.

Before long, I made more runs. I could barely afford them, but by the 4th trip, I had caught the attention of the director, who graciously provided all I needed at no cost from that time on.

Everything was going so well…

Then the unexpected happened…

The local priests got wind of the meetings. They were outraged…a strange reaction. They began to seek out those who came to the house for Bible study. They proceeded to go from house to house confiscating the Testaments.

What happened next was beyond comprehension! Picture the scene…the old houses were heated with wood. Every house had a wood burning stove with a kettle of hot water on top. The priest would gather the family around the stove and lecture them sternly against the danger of having Bibles in their possession. He lifted the stove lid and thrust the Bibles into the flames.

They were told they were too ignorant to handle the word of God…strictly forbidden to own one!

Then they were forbidden to come to my house and if I was to visit their homes, they were instructed to take the kettle of boiling water from the stove and fling it in my face…or, better yet, between my legs!!

Unbelievable vitriol! Instead of being glad for the changes in their young people's lives, they were enraged and went on the attack.

As time went on, they tried to have me deported (unsuccessfully), threatened to burn my house to the ground, openly incited the people against me with the remark "We can't be held responsible for what they might do…"

It was outrageous and out of all proportion…a witch hunt!

How could this be happening in modern times?

It all seemed like something out of the dark ages.

I got a burr under my saddle, as they say.

I went straight out and got more Bibles for the kids.

They just got better at hiding them! And we continued on.

Then a moment of revelation….

A few years before, when I had brought a Bible to my father's home for the 1st time, he had the most extraordinary reaction.

I was 22, he was nearly 50. He was French-Canadian and Catholic.

When I showed it to him, wanting him to read an especially beautiful passage, he recoiled in abject horror and ordered me…and the Bible…out of the house! Never had I seen him so frightened and panic-stricken!

There was no reasoning with him.

I never understood it…until these experiences.

In his childhood, they had been strictly forbidden to have contact with a Bible.

"Aren't these people supposed to be Christian!?" I wondered.

These isolated communities were rife with the kind of abuse that should have been unthinkable in this day and age.

As time went on, I heard stories of sexual abuse of altar boys, vulnerable women, housekeepers and nuns.

The front door of each house was reserved for the annual visit of the priest who would lean hard on the families for money.

They were held in such fear and esteem that they even had the right of the bride on her wedding night. Until recent times, the church had exercised control over all commerce.

If you needed a bolt of fabric, a barrel of molasses or flour, salt, etc. you got it through the basement of the church. They controlled everything.

Our innocently undertaken Bible studies were more of a threat than I realized. It was not planned, but the gauntlet had been thrown down…

www.ingramcontent.com/pod-product-compliance
Lightning Source LLC
Chambersburg PA
CBHW021748150726
47989CB00004B/1566